JESUS: THE LIGHT OF THE WORLD

A Study of the Gospel According to John

Dr. Tracy L. Marrs, Ed.D.

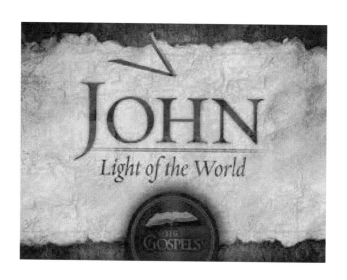

Starting Date: _____

Ending Date: _____

Name: _____

Phone: _____

Email: _____

About
This Journal

The gospel according to John was written by John the apostle. John was aware of the first three gospels written by Matthew, Mark, and Luke and his intention for writing this book was not to take away from anything presented in the previous gospel. Rather, John wanted to provide a complementary account from his personal perspective.

The book of John presents additional details to complement the other gospel books, which help provide us with understanding specific events that took place during the ministry of Jesus. John includes information that are not found in the other gospels and provides supplemental details to help increase our understanding in a complementary way without compromising the validity of the other gospels.

I believe you will gain an increasing understanding of the life, mission, and ministry of Jesus as you study the gospel according to John. Take your time reading through each passage and allow the Holy Spirit guide you with understanding the Word of God.

SOAP IT UP!! Get in the WORD and stay in the WORD!!!!

How

to Use This Journal

S

Scripture - Write It!

Read your Scripture, then write in your journal the
Verse(s) that stand out.

O

Observation - Think It!

What do you think God was saying to the people He
wrote the book to?
Rewrite the Scripture in your own words.
Consult your commentary for help.

A

Application - Live It!

Personalize what you've read by asking yourself how it
applies to your life.
Is it an instruction? An encouragement? A promise?
A call to take corrective action?
Write how this Scripture applies to you today.
Use "I Will" statements and "I Know" statements!

P

Prayer - Say It!

Your prayer can be as simple as asking God to help you
use this Scripture, praising him for something He's
done, or confessing a sin.
Write it out, just like you would an email, text or letter.

Then live it out!

How
to Spread God's Word

Spread God's Word: share the SOAP method with others!

Here's how:

1. Pray that God will lead you to people willing to receive His Word.

2. Ask them to meet with you to study the Bible. Pick a convenient time and location.

3. Share examples from your SOAP journal, then show them some Verses to SOAP on their own.

4. Spend 10 minutes hanging out, 10 minutes SOAPing, and 10 minutes in discussion and prayer (30 minutes total).

Reading Plan

The following reading plan will guide you through the book of John. Try your best to stick to the reading for each day. If you miss a day or two, don't stop. Pick back up and keep pressing into God's Word.

Week 1

Day 1 - John 1:1-5
Day 2 - John 1:6-13
Day 3 - John 1:14-18
Day 4 - John 1:19-34
Day 5 - John 1:35-51

Week 2

Day 1 - John 2:1-12
Day 2 - John 2:13-25
Day 3 - John 3:1-21
Day 4 - John 3:22-36
Day 5 - Catch-Up

Week 3

Day 1 - John 4:1-6
Day 2 - John 4:7-38
Day 3 - John 4:39-45
Day 4 - John 4:46-54
Day 5 - John 5:1-17

Week 4

Day 1 - John 5:18-24
Day 2 - John 5:25-32
Day 3 - John 5:33-47
Day 4 - John 6:1-14
Day 5 - Catch-Up

Week 5

Day 1 - John 6:15-25
Day 2 - John 6:26-40
Day 3 - John 6:41-58
Day 4 - John 6:59-65
Day 5 - John 6:66-71

Week 6

Day 1 - John 7:1-39
Day 2 - John 7:40-53
Day 3 - John 8:1-11
Day 4 - John 8:12-30
Day 5 - John 8:31-59

Week 7

Day 1 - John 9:1-12
Day 2 - John 9:13-34
Day 3 - John 9:35-41
Day 4 - John 10:1-21
Day 5 - John 10:22-42

Week 8

Day 1 - John 11:1-46
Day 2 - John 11:47-57
Day 3 - John 12:1-11
Day 4 - John 12:12-19
Day 5 - Catch-Up

Reading Plan Cont.

Week 9

Day 1 - John 12:20-26
Day 2 - John 12:27-50
Day 3 - John 13:1-4
Day 4 - John 13:5-20
Day 5 - John 13:21-38

Week 10

Day 1 - John 14:1-6
Day 2 - John 14:7-15
Day 3 - John 14:16-31
Day 4 - John 15:1-11
Day 5 - Catch-Up

Week 11

Day 1 - John 15:12-17
Day 2 - John 15:18-27
Day 3 - John 16:1-4
Day 4 - John 16:5-15
Day 5 - John 16:16-22

Week 12

Day 1 - John 16:23-33
Day 2 - John 17:1-12
Day 3 - John 17:13-21
Day 4 - John 17:22-26
Day 5 - John 18:1-11

Week 13

Day 1 - John 18:12-24
Day 2 - John 18:25-27
Day 3 - John 18:28-40
Day 4 - John 19:1-15
Day 5 - Catch-Up

Thoughts/Prayers Before Beginning:

_____

_____

_____

_____

_____

_____

_____

_____

_____

_____

_____

_____

_____

_____

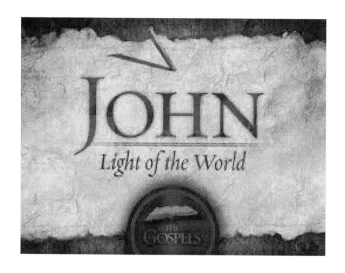

Week One

Weekly Focus Verse

In the beginning was the Word, and the Word was with God, and the Word was God. He was with God in the beginning. Through Him all things were made; without Him nothing was made that has been made.

John 1:1-3

Day 1
Today's Reading: John 1:1-5

S _In Him was life and the life_
was the light of men.

O _I believe that he is_
wanting us to live the way He
wants us to!

A _I'm going to start living and listening to what He wants me to._

P _Lord please lead me in the Right direction._

Weekly Focus Verse

Day 2
Today's Reading: John 1:6-13

S _He came whto his own and his own received Him not._

O _He's saying He sent Him Down to earth for a reason._

A _I'm going to start listening to god more often._

P _God give me a sign that this is what you want me to do._

Weekly Focus Verse

John 15

Day 3

Today's Reading: John 1:14-18

S _For the law was was given by Moses but grace and Truth came by Jesus Christ._

O _He had Moses right. the laws down a we med to follow them._

A _I'm going to follow the Laws the best I can._

P _Lord please Help me through the Hard times._

Weekly Focus Verse

Day 4
Today's Reading: John 1:19-34

S _____

_____

_____

_____

_____

_____

_____

_____

O _____

_____

_____

_____

_____

_____

_____

_____

A _____

_____

_____

_____

_____

_____

P _____

_____

_____

_____

_____

_____

Weekly Focus Verse

_____

_____

_____

_____

_____

Day 5

Today's Reading: John 1:35-51

S _____

_____

_____

_____

_____

_____

_____

O _____

_____

_____

_____

_____

_____

_____

_____

A _____

_____

_____

_____

_____

_____

P _____

_____

_____

_____

_____

_____

Weekly Focus Verse

_____

_____

_____

_____

_____

Saturday:

Look back at all God has pointed out to you this week while SOAPIng and record the one passage that God really spoke to your heart about.

_____

_____

_____

_____

_____

_____

_____

_____

_____

_____

_____

_____

_____

_____

Sunday:

It's Sunday; time to worship with God's family! Use this page to take down what you hear from God through His Word today! Take a moment to pray for GBC!

_____

_____

_____

_____

_____

_____

_____

_____

_____

_____

_____

_____

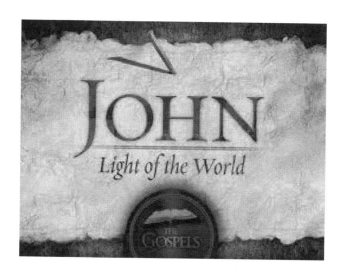

Week Two

Weekly Focus Verse

Jesus replied, "Very truly I tell you, no one can see the kingdom of God unless they are born again."

John 3:3

Day 1

Today's Reading: John 2:1-12

S _____

_____

_____

_____

_____

_____

_____

O _____

_____

_____

_____

_____

_____

_____

_____

A _____

_____

_____

_____

_____

_____

P _____

_____

_____

_____

Weekly Focus Verse

_____
_____
_____
_____
_____
_____
_____

Day 2
Today's Reading: John 2:13-25

S _____

_____

_____

_____

_____

_____

O _____

_____

_____

_____

_____

_____

_____

_____

A _____

_____

_____

_____

_____

_____

P _____

_____

_____

_____

_____

_____

Weekly Focus Verse

_____

_____

_____

_____

_____

Day 3

Today's Reading: John 3:1-21

S _____

_____

_____

_____

_____

_____

_____

O _____

_____

_____

_____

_____

_____

_____

_____

_____

A _____

_____

_____

_____

_____

_____

P _____

_____

_____

_____

_____

Weekly Focus Verse

_____

_____

_____

_____

_____

_____

Day 4

Today's Reading: John 3:22-36

S _____

_____

_____

_____

_____

_____

_____

O _____

_____

_____

_____

_____

_____

_____

_____

A _____

_____

_____

_____

_____

_____

P _____

_____

_____

_____

_____

Weekly Focus Verse

_____
_____
_____
_____
_____
_____

Day 5
Today's Reading: Catch-Up

S _____

_____

_____

_____

_____

_____

_____

O _____

_____

_____

_____

_____

_____

_____

_____

_____

A _____

_____

_____

_____

_____

_____

_____

P _____

_____

_____

_____

_____

Weekly Focus Verse

_____

_____

_____

_____

_____

_____

_____

Saturday:

Look back at all God has pointed out to you this week while SOAPIng and record the one passage that God really spoke to your heart about.

_____

_____

_____

_____

_____

_____

_____

_____

_____

_____

_____

_____

_____

_____

Sunday:

It's Sunday; time to worship with God's family! Use this page to take down what you hear from God through His Word today! Take a moment to pray for GBC!

_____

_____

_____

_____

_____

_____

_____

_____

_____

_____

_____

_____

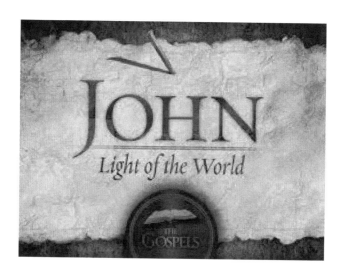

Week Three

Weekly Focus Verse

"But whoever drinks the water I give them will never thirst. Indeed, the water I give will become in them a spring of water welling up to eternal life."

John 4:14

Day 1
Today's Reading: John 4:1-6

S _____

_____

_____

_____

_____

O _____

_____

_____

_____

_____

_____

_____

_____

_____

_____

A _____

_____

_____

_____

_____

_____

P _____

_____

_____

_____

Weekly Focus Verse

_____

_____

_____

_____

_____

_____

Day 2
Today's Reading: John 4:7-38

S _____

_____

_____

_____

_____

_____

_____

O _____

_____

_____

_____

_____

_____

_____

_____

_____

A _____

_____

_____

_____

_____

_____

P _____

_____

_____

_____

_____

Weekly Focus Verse

_____

_____

_____

_____

_____

_____

_____

Day 3
Today's Reading: John 4:39-45

S _____

_____

_____

_____

_____

_____

_____

O _____

_____

_____

_____

_____

_____

_____

_____

A _____

_____

_____

_____

_____

_____

P _____

_____

_____

_____

_____

Weekly Focus Verse

_____

_____

_____

_____

_____

_____

John

Day 4

Today's Reading: John 4:46-54

S _____

_____

_____

_____

_____

_____

_____

O _____

_____

_____

_____

_____

_____

_____

_____

A _____

_____

_____

_____

_____

_____

P _____

_____

_____

_____

_____

Weekly Focus Verse

_____

_____

_____

_____

_____

_____

John

Day 5
Today's Reading: John 5:1-17

S _____

_____

_____

_____

_____

_____

O _____

_____

_____

_____

_____

_____

_____

_____

A _____

_____

_____

_____

_____

_____

P _____

_____

_____

_____

_____

Weekly Focus Verse

_____

_____

_____

_____

_____

_____

Saturday:

Look back at all God has pointed out to you this week while SOAPIng and record the one passage that God really spoke to your heart about.

_____

_____

_____

_____

_____

_____

_____

_____

_____

_____

_____

_____

_____

Sunday:

It's Sunday; time to worship with God's family! Use this page to take down what you hear from God through His Word today! Take a moment to pray for GBC!

_____

_____

_____

_____

_____

_____

_____

_____

_____

_____

_____

_____

_____

John

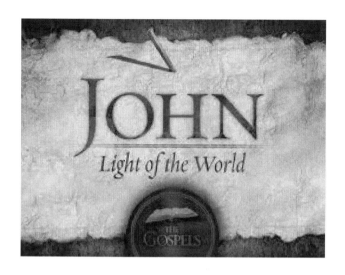

Week Four

Weekly Focus Verse

"Very truly I tell you, whoever hears my word and believes him who sent me has eternal life and will not be judged but has crossed over from death to life."

John 5:24

Day 1
Today's Reading: John 5:18-24

S _____

_____

_____

_____

_____

_____

_____

O _____

_____

_____

_____

_____

_____

_____

_____

_____

A _____

_____

_____

_____

_____

_____

_____

P _____

_____

_____

_____

_____

Weekly Focus Verse

_____

_____

_____

_____

_____

_____

_____

Day 2
Today's Reading: John 5:25-32

S _____

_____

_____

_____

_____

_____

_____

O _____

_____

_____

_____

_____

_____

_____

_____

A _____

_____

_____

_____

_____

_____

P _____

_____

_____

_____

_____

Weekly Focus Verse

_____

_____

_____

_____

_____

_____

Day 3

Today's Reading: John 5:33-47

S _____

_____

_____

_____

_____

_____

_____

O _____

_____

_____

_____

_____

_____

_____

_____

A _____

_____

_____

_____

_____

_____

P _____

_____

_____

_____

_____

Weekly Focus Verse

_____

_____

_____

_____

_____

_____

_____

John

Day 4

Today's Reading: John 6:1-14

S _____

_____

_____

_____

_____

_____

_____

O _____

_____

_____

_____

_____

_____

_____

_____

_____

A _____

_____

_____

_____

_____

_____

P _____

_____

_____

_____

_____

Weekly Focus Verse

_____

_____

_____

_____

_____

_____

John

Day 5
Today's Reading: Catch-Up

S _____

_____

_____

_____

_____

_____

_____

O _____

_____

_____

_____

_____

_____

_____

_____

_____

A _____

_____

_____

_____

_____

_____

_____

P _____

_____

_____

_____

_____

_____

Weekly Focus Verse

_____

_____

_____

_____

_____

_____

_____

Saturday:

Look back at all God has pointed out to you this week while SOAPIng and record the one passage that God really spoke to your heart about.

_____

_____

_____

_____

_____

_____

_____

_____

_____

_____

_____

_____

_____

_____

_____

Sunday:

It's Sunday; time to worship with God's family! Use this page to take down what you hear from God through His Word today! Take a moment to pray for GBC!

_____

_____

_____

_____

_____

_____

_____

_____

_____

_____

_____

_____

_____

John

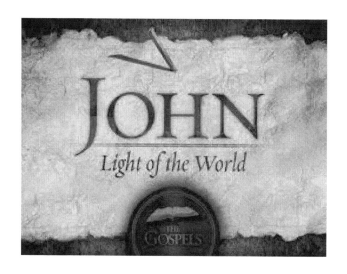

Week Five

Weekly Focus Verse

Then Jesus declared, "I am the bread of life. Whoever comes to me will never to hungry, and whoever believes in me will never be thirsty."

John 6:35

Day 1
Today's Reading: John 6:15-25

S _____

_____

_____

_____

_____

_____

_____

O _____

_____

_____

_____

_____

_____

_____

_____

_____

A _____

_____

_____

_____

_____

_____

P _____

_____

_____

_____

Weekly Focus Verse

_____

_____

_____

_____

_____

_____

_____

Day 2
Today's Reading: John 6:26-40

S _____

_____

_____

_____

_____

_____

_____

O _____

_____

_____

_____

_____

_____

_____

_____

_____

A _____

_____

_____

_____

_____

_____

P _____

_____

_____

_____

_____

_____

Weekly Focus Verse

_____

_____

_____

_____

_____

_____

Day 3

Today's Reading: John 6:41-58

S _____

_____

_____

_____

_____

_____

_____

O _____

_____

_____

_____

_____

_____

_____

_____

A _____

_____

_____

_____

_____

_____

P _____

_____

_____

_____

Weekly Focus Verse

_____

_____

_____

_____

_____

_____

John

Day 4
Today's Reading: John 6:59-65

S _____

_____

_____

_____

_____

_____

_____

O _____

_____

_____

_____

_____

_____

_____

_____

_____

A _____

_____

_____

_____

_____

_____

P _____

_____

_____

_____

_____

_____

Weekly Focus Verse

_____

_____

_____

_____

_____

_____

_____

Day 5
Today's Reading: John 6:66-71

S _____

_____

_____

_____

_____

_____

_____

O _____

_____

_____

_____

_____

_____

_____

_____

_____

A _____

_____

_____

_____

_____

_____

P _____

_____

_____

_____

_____

Weekly Focus Verse

_____

_____

_____

_____

_____

_____

_____

John

Saturday:

Look back at all God has pointed out to you this week while SOAPIng and record the one passage that God really spoke to your heart about.

_____

_____

_____

_____

_____

_____

_____

_____

_____

_____

_____

_____

_____

Sunday:

It's Sunday; time to worship with God's family! Use this page to take down what you hear from God through His Word today! Take a moment to pray for GBC!

_____

_____

_____

_____

_____

_____

_____

_____

_____

_____

_____

_____

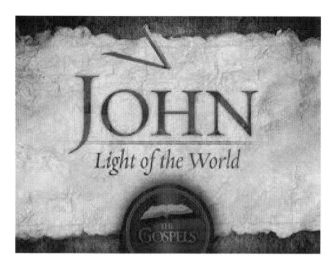

Week Six

Weekly Focus Verse

On the last and greatest day of the festival, Jesus stood and said in a loud voice, "Let anyone who is thirsty come to me and drink. Whoever believes in me, as Scripture has said, rivers of living water will flow from within them."

John 7:37-38

Day 1
Today's Reading: John 7:1-39

S _____

_____

_____

_____

_____

_____

_____

O _____

_____

_____

_____

_____

_____

_____

_____

A _____

_____

_____

_____

_____

P _____

_____

_____

_____

_____

Weekly Focus Verse

_____

_____

_____

_____

_____

_____

_____

Day 2
Today's Reading: John 7:40-53

S _____

_____

_____

_____

_____

_____

_____

O _____

_____

_____

_____

_____

_____

_____

A _____

_____

_____

_____

_____

_____

_____

P _____

_____

_____

_____

_____

Weekly Focus Verse

_____

_____

_____

_____

_____

_____

Day 3
Today's Reading: John 8:1-11

S _____

_____

_____

_____

_____

_____

_____

O _____

_____

_____

_____

_____

_____

_____

_____

A _____

_____

_____

_____

_____

_____

_____

_____

P _____

_____

_____

_____

_____

Weekly Focus Verse

_____

_____

_____

_____

_____

_____

Day 4
Today's Reading: John 8:12-30

S _____

_____

_____

_____

_____

_____

_____

O _____

_____

_____

_____

_____

_____

_____

_____

A _____

_____

_____

_____

_____

_____

P _____

_____

_____

_____

_____

_____

Weekly Focus Verse

_____

_____

_____

_____

_____

Day 5

Today's Reading: John 8:31-59

S _____

_____

_____

_____

_____

_____

_____

O _____

_____

_____

_____

_____

_____

_____

_____

_____

A _____

_____

_____

_____

_____

_____

P _____

_____

_____

_____

_____

_____

Weekly Focus Verse

_____

_____

_____

_____

_____

Saturday:

Look back at all God has pointed out to you this week while SOAPIng and record the one passage that God really spoke to your heart about.

_____

_____

_____

_____

_____

_____

_____

_____

_____

_____

_____

_____

_____

Sunday:

It's Sunday; time to worship with God's family! Use this page to take down what you hear from God through His Word today! Take a moment to pray for GBC!

_____

_____

_____

_____

_____

_____

_____

_____

_____

_____

_____

_____

_____

John   93

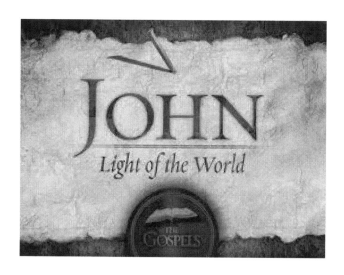

Week Seven

Weekly Focus Verse

"I am the good shepherd. The good shepherd lays down his life for the sheep."

John 10:11

Day 1

Today's Reading: John 9:1-12

S _____

_____

_____

_____

_____

_____

_____

O _____

_____

_____

_____

_____

_____

_____

_____

A _____

_____

_____

_____

_____

_____

P _____

_____

_____

_____

_____

_____

Weekly Focus Verse

_____

_____

_____

_____

_____

_____

_____

Day 2
Today's Reading: John 9:13-34

S _____

_____

_____

_____

_____

_____

_____

O _____

_____

_____

_____

_____

_____

_____

_____

A _____

_____

_____

_____

_____

_____

P _____

_____

_____

_____

_____

_____

Weekly Focus Verse

_____

_____

_____

_____

_____

_____

Day 3

Today's Reading: John 9:35-41

S _____

_____

_____

_____

_____

_____

_____

O _____

_____

_____

_____

_____

_____

_____

_____

A _____

_____

_____

_____

_____

_____

_____

P _____

_____

_____

_____

_____

_____

Weekly Focus Verse

_____

_____

_____

_____

_____

_____

_____

Day 4
Today's Reading: John 10:1-21

S _____

_____

_____

_____

_____

_____

_____

O _____

_____

_____

_____

_____

_____

_____

_____

_____

A _____

_____

_____

_____

_____

_____

_____

P _____

_____

_____

_____

_____

Weekly Focus Verse

_____

_____

_____

_____

_____

_____

Day 5
Today's Reading: John 10:22-42

S _____

_____

_____

_____

_____

_____

_____

O _____

_____

_____

_____

_____

_____

_____

_____

_____

A _____

_____

_____

_____

_____

_____

P _____

_____

_____

_____

_____

Weekly Focus Verse

_____
_____
_____
_____
_____
_____
_____

Saturday:

Look back at all God has pointed out to you this week while SOAPIng and record the one passage that God really spoke to your heart about.

_____

_____

_____

_____

_____

_____

_____

_____

_____

_____

_____

_____

_____

Sunday:

It's Sunday; time to worship with God's family! Use this page to take down what you hear from God through His Word today! Take a moment to pray for GBC!

_____

_____

_____

_____

_____

_____

_____

_____

_____

_____

_____

_____

_____

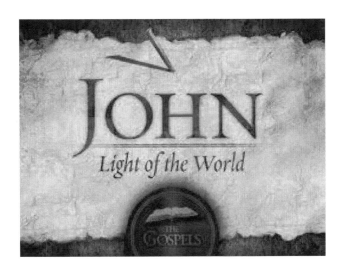

Week Eight

Weekly Focus Verse

Jesus said to her, "I am the resurrection and the life. The one who believes in me will live, even though they die; and whoever lives by believing in me will never die. Do you believe this?"

John 11:25-26

Day 1

Today's Reading: John 11:1-46

S _____

_____

_____

_____

_____

O _____

_____

_____

_____

_____

_____

_____

_____

_____

_____

A _____

_____

_____

_____

_____

_____

P _____

_____

_____

_____

_____

Weekly Focus Verse

_____
_____
_____
_____
_____
_____
_____

Day 2

Today's Reading: John 11:47-57

S _____

_____

_____

_____

_____

_____

_____

O _____

_____

_____

_____

_____

_____

_____

_____

A _____

_____

_____

_____

_____

_____

P _____

_____

_____

_____

_____

Weekly Focus Verse

_____

_____

_____

_____

_____

_____

Day 3
Today's Reading: John 12:1-11

S _____

_____

_____

_____

_____

_____

O _____

_____

_____

_____

_____

_____

_____

_____

A _____

_____

_____

_____

_____

_____

P _____

_____

_____

_____

_____

Weekly Focus Verse

_____

_____

_____

_____

_____

_____

Day 4

Today's Reading: John 12:12-19

S _____

_____

_____

_____

_____

_____

O _____

_____

_____

_____

_____

_____

_____

_____

A _____

_____

_____

_____

_____

_____

_____

P _____

_____

_____

_____

_____

Weekly Focus Verse

_____

_____

_____

_____

_____

_____

Day 5
Today's Reading: Catch-Up

S _____

_____

_____

_____

_____

_____

O _____

_____

_____

_____

_____

_____

_____

_____

A _____

_____

_____

_____

_____

_____

_____

P _____

_____

_____

_____

_____

_____

Weekly Focus Verse

_____

_____

_____

_____

_____

_____

_____

Saturday:

Look back at all God has pointed out to you this week while SOAPIng and record the one passage that God really spoke to your heart about.

_____

_____

_____

_____

_____

_____

_____

_____

_____

_____

_____

_____

_____

Sunday:

It's Sunday; time to worship with God's family! Use this page to take down what you hear from God through His Word today! Take a moment to pray for GBC!

_____

_____

_____

_____

_____

_____

_____

_____

_____

_____

_____

_____

_____

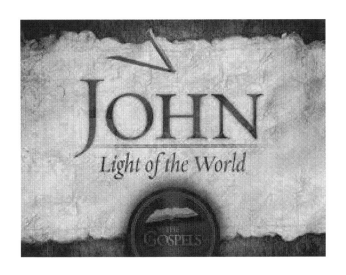

Week Nine

Weekly Focus Verse

"Whoever serves me must follow me; and where I am, my servant also will be. My Father will honor the one who serves me."

John 12:26

Week Nine

Day 1
Today's Reading: John 12:20-26

S _____

_____

_____

_____

_____

_____

_____

O _____

_____

_____

_____

_____

_____

_____

_____

_____

_____

A _____

_____

_____

_____

_____

_____

P _____

_____

_____

_____

_____

Weekly Focus Verse

_____

_____

_____

_____

_____

_____

Day 2

Today's Reading: John 12:27-50

S _____

_____

_____

_____

_____

_____

_____

O _____

_____

_____

_____

_____

_____

_____

_____

A _____

_____

_____

_____

_____

_____

_____

P _____

_____

_____

_____

_____

_____

Weekly Focus Verse

_____

_____

_____

_____

_____

_____

_____

Day 3
Today's Reading: John 13:1-4

S _____

_____

_____

_____

_____

_____

_____

O _____

_____

_____

_____

_____

_____

_____

_____

_____

A _____

_____

_____

_____

_____

_____

P _____

_____

_____

_____

_____

Weekly Focus Verse

_____

_____

_____

_____

_____

_____

_____

Day 4
Today's Reading: John 13:5-20

S _____

_____

_____

_____

_____

_____

_____

O _____

_____

_____

_____

_____

_____

_____

_____

_____

A _____

_____

_____

_____

_____

_____

P _____

_____

_____

_____

_____

Weekly Focus Verse

_____

_____

_____

_____

_____

_____

Day 5
Today's Reading: John 13:21-38

S _____

_____

_____

_____

_____

_____

_____

O _____

_____

_____

_____

_____

_____

_____

_____

_____

A _____

_____

_____

_____

_____

_____

_____

P _____

_____

_____

_____

_____

Weekly Focus Verse

_____

_____

_____

_____

_____

_____

_____

Saturday:

Look back at all God has pointed out to you this week while SOAPIng and record the one passage that God really spoke to your heart about.

_____

_____

_____

_____

_____

_____

_____

_____

_____

_____

_____

_____

_____

Sunday:

It's Sunday; time to worship with God's family! Use this page to take down what you hear from God through His Word today! Take a moment to pray for GBC!

_____

_____

_____

_____

_____

_____

_____

_____

_____

_____

_____

_____

_____

_____

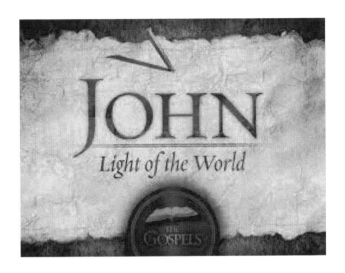

Week Ten

Weekly Focus Verse

Jesus answered, "I am the way and the truth and the life. No one comes to the Father except through me."

John 14:6

Day 1

Today's Reading: John 14:1-6

S _____

_____

_____

_____

_____

_____

_____

O _____

_____

_____

_____

_____

_____

_____

_____

_____

A _____

_____

_____

_____

_____

_____

_____

P _____

_____

_____

_____

_____

_____

Weekly Focus Verse

_____

_____

_____

_____

_____

_____

_____

Day 2
Today's Reading: John 14:7-15

S _____

_____

_____

_____

_____

_____

O _____

_____

_____

_____

_____

_____

_____

_____

A _____

_____

_____

_____

_____

_____

_____

P _____

_____

_____

_____

_____

_____

Weekly Focus Verse

_____

_____

_____

_____

_____

_____

Day 3
Today's Reading: John 14:16-31

S _____

_____

_____

_____

_____

_____

_____

O _____

_____

_____

_____

_____

_____

_____

_____

_____

A _____

_____

_____

_____

_____

_____

P _____

_____

_____

_____

_____

Weekly Focus Verse

_____

_____

_____

_____

_____

_____

Day 4

Today's Reading: John 15:1-11

S _____

_____

_____

_____

_____

_____

_____

O _____

_____

_____

_____

_____

_____

_____

_____

_____

A _____

_____

_____

_____

_____

_____

_____

P _____

_____

_____

_____

_____

Weekly Focus Verse

_____

_____

_____

_____

_____

_____

_____

Day 5
Today's Reading: Catch-Up

S _____

_____

_____

_____

_____

_____

O _____

_____

_____

_____

_____

_____

_____

_____

A _____

_____

_____

_____

_____

_____

_____

P _____

_____

_____

_____

_____

Weekly Focus Verse

_____

_____

_____

_____

_____

_____

_____

Saturday:

Look back at all God has pointed out to you this week while SOAPIng and record the one passage that God really spoke to your heart about.

_____

_____

_____

_____

_____

_____

_____

_____

_____

_____

_____

_____

_____

_____

Sunday:

It's Sunday; time to worship with God's family! Use this page to take down what you hear from God through His Word today! Take a moment to pray for GBC!

_____

_____

_____

_____

_____

_____

_____

_____

_____

_____

_____

_____

_____

_____

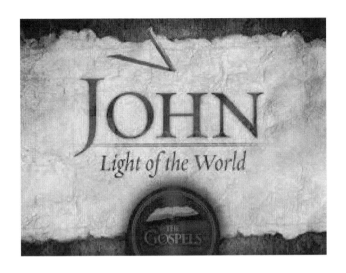

Week Eleven

Weekly Focus Verse

"I am the vine; you are the branches. If you remain in me and I in you, you will bear much fruit; apart from me you can do nothing."

John 15:5

Day 1

Today's Reading: John 15:12-17

S _____

_____

_____

_____

_____

_____

_____

O _____

_____

_____

_____

_____

_____

_____

_____

A _____

_____

_____

_____

_____

_____

_____

P _____

_____

_____

_____

_____

Weekly Focus Verse

_____

_____

_____

_____

_____

_____

_____

Day 2

Today's Reading: John 15:18-27

S _____

_____

_____

_____

_____

_____

_____

O _____

_____

_____

_____

_____

_____

_____

_____

_____

A _____

_____

_____

_____

_____

_____

_____

P _____

_____

_____

_____

_____

Weekly Focus Verse

_____

_____

_____

_____

_____

_____

_____

Day 3

Today's Reading: John 16:1-4

S _____

_____

_____

_____

_____

_____

_____

O _____

_____

_____

_____

_____

_____

_____

_____

_____

A _____

_____

_____

_____

_____

_____

_____

P _____

_____

_____

_____

_____

Weekly Focus Verse

_____
_____
_____
_____
_____
_____

Day 4
Today's Reading: John 16:5-15

S _____

_____

_____

_____

_____

_____

_____

O _____

_____

_____

_____

_____

_____

_____

_____

_____

A _____

_____

_____

_____

_____

_____

P _____

_____

_____

_____

_____

Weekly Focus Verse

_____

_____

_____

_____

_____

_____

Day 5

Today's Reading: John 16:16-22

S _____

_____

_____

_____

_____

_____

O _____

_____

_____

_____

_____

_____

_____

_____

A _____

_____

_____

_____

_____

_____

P _____

_____

_____

_____

_____

Weekly Focus Verse

_____

_____

_____

_____

_____

_____

_____

Saturday:

Look back at all God has pointed out to you this week while SOAPIng and record the one passage that God really spoke to your heart about.

_____

_____

_____

_____

_____

_____

_____

_____

_____

_____

_____

_____

_____

Sunday:

It's Sunday; time to worship with God's family! Use this page to take down what you hear from God through His Word today! Take a moment to pray for GBC!

_____

_____

_____

_____

_____

_____

_____

_____

_____

_____

_____

_____

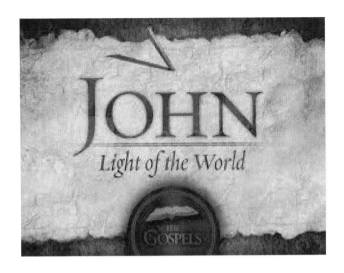

Week Twelve

Weekly Focus Verse

After Jesus said this, he looked toward heaven and prayed: "Father, the hour has come. Glorify your Son, that your Son may glorify you."

John 17:1

Day 1

Today's Reading: John 16:23-33

S _____

_____

_____

_____

_____

_____

_____

O _____

_____

_____

_____

_____

_____

_____

A _____

_____

_____

_____

_____

_____

_____

P _____

_____

_____

_____

_____

Weekly Focus Verse

_____

_____

_____

_____

_____

_____

Day 2

Today's Reading: John 17:1-12

S _____

_____

_____

_____

_____

_____

O _____

_____

_____

_____

_____

_____

_____

_____

A _____

_____

_____

_____

_____

_____

_____

P _____

_____

_____

_____

_____

_____

Weekly Focus Verse

_____

_____

_____

_____

_____

_____

John   169

Day 3
Today's Reading: John 17:13-21

S _____

_____

_____

_____

_____

_____

_____

O _____

_____

_____

_____

_____

_____

_____

_____

_____

_____

Week Twelve

A _____

_____

_____

_____

_____

_____

P _____

_____

_____

_____

Weekly Focus Verse

_____

_____

_____

_____

_____

_____

John
171

Day 4

Today's Reading: John 17:22-26

S _____

_____

_____

_____

_____

_____

_____

O _____

_____

_____

_____

_____

_____

_____

_____

_____

A _____

_____

_____

_____

_____

_____

_____

P _____

_____

_____

_____

_____

Weekly Focus Verse

_____

_____

_____

_____

_____

_____

_____

Day 5

Today's Reading: John 18:1-11

S _____

_____

_____

_____

_____

_____

_____

O _____

_____

_____

_____

_____

_____

_____

_____

_____

A _____

_____

_____

_____

_____

_____

P _____

_____

_____

_____

_____

Weekly Focus Verse

_____

_____

_____

_____

_____

_____

Saturday:

Look back at all God has pointed out to you this week while SOAPIng and record the one passage that God really spoke to your heart about.

_____

_____

_____

_____

_____

_____

_____

_____

_____

_____

_____

_____

_____

Sunday:

It's Sunday; time to worship with God's family! Use this page to take down what you hear from God through His Word today! Take a moment to pray for GBC!

_____

_____

_____

_____

_____

_____

_____

_____

_____

_____

_____

_____

_____

_____

Week Thirteen

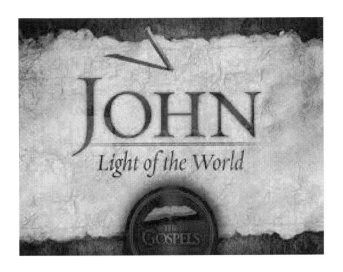

Week Thirteen

Weekly Focus Verse

"You are a king, then!" said Pilate. Jesus answered, "You say that I am a king. In fact, the reason I was born and came into the world is to testify to the truth. Everyone on the side of truth listens to me."

John 18:37

Day 1

Today's Reading: John 18:12-24

S _____

_____

_____

_____

_____

_____

_____

O _____

_____

_____

_____

_____

_____

_____

_____

A _____

_____

_____

_____

_____

_____

_____

P _____

_____

_____

_____

_____

Weekly Focus Verse

_____

_____

_____

_____

_____

_____

Day 2

Today's Reading: John 18:25-27

S _____

_____

_____

_____

_____

_____

_____

O _____

_____

_____

_____

_____

_____

_____

_____

_____

A _____

_____

_____

_____

_____

_____

_____

P _____

_____

_____

_____

_____

_____

Weekly Focus Verse

_____

_____

_____

_____

_____

_____

Day 3

Today's Reading: John 18:28-40

S _____

_____

_____

_____

_____

_____

_____

O _____

_____

_____

_____

_____

_____

_____

_____

A _____

_____

_____

_____

_____

_____

_____

P _____

_____

_____

_____

_____

Weekly Focus Verse

_____

_____

_____

_____

_____

_____

Day 4

Today's Reading: John 19:1-15

S _____

_____

_____

_____

_____

_____

_____

O _____

_____

_____

_____

_____

_____

_____

_____

A _____

_____

_____

_____

_____

_____

P _____

_____

_____

_____

_____

Weekly Focus Verse

_____

_____

_____

_____

_____

_____

Day 5

Today's Reading: Catch-Up

S _____

_____

_____

_____

_____

_____

O _____

_____

_____

_____

_____

_____

_____

_____

A _____

_____

_____

_____

_____

_____

_____

P _____

_____

_____

_____

_____

Weekly Focus Verse

_____

_____

_____

_____

_____

_____

_____

Saturday:

Look back at all God has pointed out to you this week while SOAPIng and record the one passage that God really spoke to your heart about.

_____

_____

_____

_____

_____

_____

_____

_____

_____

_____

_____

_____

Sunday:

It's Sunday; time to worship with God's family! Use this page to take down what you hear from God through His Word today! Take a moment to pray for GBC!

_____

_____

_____

_____

_____

_____

_____

_____

_____

_____

_____

_____

_____

_____

Week Thirteen

Notes:

_____

_____

_____

_____

_____

_____

_____

_____

_____

_____

_____

_____

_____

_____

_____

_____

_____

John

Notes:

_____

_____

_____

_____

_____

_____

_____

_____

_____

_____

_____

_____

_____

_____

_____

_____